£1

C000118678

Oliver Reynolds was born in 1957, in Cardiff, and grew up there. After taking a drama degree at Hull University, he returned home to work in the theatre (adapting *Sinbad* for puppets and *The Snow Queen* for pantomime). In 1985, he won the Arvon International Poetry Prize. Having been writer in residence at the Universities of Cambridge, Glasgow and Strathclyde, he now lives in London.

Faber and Faber have published two volumes of his poetry, *Skevington's Daughter* (1985) and *The Player Queen's Wife* (1987).

by the same author

SKEVINGTON'S DAUGHTER
THE PLAYER QUEEN'S WIFE

THE OSLO TRAM
Oliver Reynolds

faber and faber
LONDON · BOSTON

First published in 1991
by Faber and Faber Limited
3 Queen Square London WC1N 3AU

Photoset by Wilmaset Birkenhead Wirral
Printed in England by Clays Ltd, St Ives plc

Oliver Reynolds is hereby identified as the author of this work in
accordance with Section 77 of the Copyright, Designs and
Patents Act 1988

A CIP record for this book is available from the British Library

ISBN 0-571-15258-9

Acknowledgements

The Green Book, London Magazine, New Welsh Review, Planet, Poetry Book Society Anthology 1989–90, Poetry Wales, The Rialto, Spectator, Times Literary Supplement, Verse.

Two poems here (pages 43 and 50) are versions of poems by Rilke ('Leichen-Wäsche' and 'Spanische Tänzerin'); one (page 39) is an adaptation of Seneca (*Thyestes*, 391–403).

Med takk for trikken til Øyvind Hennestad og Hans Andreas Fristad (AS Oslo Sporveier).

Contents

for my mother

Clarinet

Such gravid cloakings
such oaky stains
How can I aged five
connect these solemnities
with the dismembered mechanism
nestling in the purple plush
of its carrying case
or with the spittly reed
fitted to its top
like a yellowed fingernail
And how did my brother Blake
a subscriber to *Meccano Magazine*
become this lone figure in a suit
in the black and white fishbowl
of a live broadcast
from the City Temple Cardiff
Why does the dark music hurt
Who's this Mozart
and why should his movement
be slow

From the Second Hell

A skein of birds
flung like a net
across the sea
of the sky
and gone
A line of men and horses
fuzzed by the dust and flies
of a summer road
One man sings in Latin
hands trailing rope
to the following rider
reins pulled by the rider in front
and a chain linking his legs
under the belly of his horse

Hoof-thuds in dry mud
and brief conversations
as the sun rests at noon
Men on foot
flank the prisoner
diagonals of pikes
whipping through leaves
Three days
for the ride to Paris
Two years
for Parliament's verdict
Captured at work
his hands are still black
with printer's ink

The silence of candles
the sifting of pages
and the shop-sign's creak
the sign of the golden axe
a cooper's axe or doloire
Madame Dolet
the printer's wife and near-widow
is checking the latest batch
from the title-page mark
of an axe
above a limb of tree
to the final-page motto
Preserve moy ò Seigneur
des calumnies des hommes

Rain at the frontier
Switzerland washes mud into France
A horse bubbles in its nose-bag
as guards stave in a barrel
and tip chestnuts into mud
Nothing like that catch at Paris
those packages branded DOLET
full of banned books
Pat as a set-up
The cart's waved on
Next morning a client inspects
a Bible in French
not quite dry
and somehow smelling of forest

The sky booms
beating pigeons from the bell-tower
In front of the cathedral
trumpets and a proclamation
a litany made up of the word
heresy
A priest walks over paving
to a heap of books
with a canister on a chain
a secular thurible
that's unlidded and spilt
Flame genuflects over a title-page
Le Nouveau Testament
imprimé par Dolet en francoys

A doormat with sleeves
his jacket's coarse and old
His lined face
is the colour of lead
as if the staple diet
of this logomach and latinist
was type
This is Étienne Dolet
charged with heresy
in his book of poems
The Second Hell
If found guilty
he will be burnt with his books
to ashes

[4]

Shut up
in the two years' limbo
of his cell
he tests the advocacy
of verse
When I've been burnt or hung
what will be left
A dead body
Will no one regret
the cruel death
of one who did no wrong
Is a man so worthless
he can be killed without thought
like a fly or a worm

Étienne Dolet
is taken in a cart
to the Place Maubert
It is 1546 and the feast-day
of Saint-Étienne
the day of Dolet's birth
thirty-eight years before
The Church likes neatness
A mound of faggots
is topped off with books
each with its first-page axe
and leafy log
The living tree
is reduced to firewood

On the Balcony

Up in the air
in our Royal Box
we can survey the fading dénouement
of last week's crash at the corner
the expressive skidmarks
and the gutter's glitter
of smashed glass
My book's unread
and smudged with sun-oil
You've a leaf on your nose
one of Titania's fairies
with her face lifted
to the spotlight of the sun
Everybody else is at work
and we're the sole occupants
of these five balconies
tiered above each other
with us on the middle one
like a little wedding couple
half-way to the top of the cake

The Oslo Tram

My death
has been timetabled
I run towards it
just as I shall run from it
on rails
As reincarnations go
mine as an Oslo tram
will be colourful
literally so
as my livery will be
an aristocratic cream
and the light blue
known in Oslo
as tram blue

It was a dream
I was as fluent
in Norwegian
as your tongue is
in my mouth
And now it's real
Here I am
word perfect
with adverts on my sides
flawlessly extolling
newspapers and chocolate
The driver
winds a handle
and destinations roll
silent and voluble
off my tongue
Sentrum
Majorstua
Frogner

Year by year
this old woman
next to the ticket punch
is translating Dostoyevsky
Night by night
she sleeps
in an iron lung
the wreck of her chest
grinding uphill
Returning from the library
she now sways
in the sunlit lung
of the tram
and turns to the chapter
in *The Devils*
where Stavrogin
bites the governor's ear

May 1st
and the flags on my roof
battle proudly
with the wind
Two old drunks in the back
belch and swear
watched in the mirror
by the driver
We stop
Slowly he stands
Look at the bass drum
of his chest
Listen to the thudding
of his walk
Shown the door
the drunks step out
into sunlight
shouting
Happy Christmas
Merry New Year
Happy Christmas

Spring has arrived
and everywhere
there's the sudden
small flail
of winter tyres on tarmac
Windows liquid with light
I'm an aquarium on wheels
and now it's your turn
to be reincarnated
on my front seat
as yourself
coming back from a swim
your hair drying
and your eyes
glazed with red
The maples outside
nurse the stumps
of their branches
Eating a croissant
you look through the window
for the first buds

Shift

The night-workers
at the mail-order warehouse
sort the last lorry-load
before the meal-break
In the locker-room
they sit without talking
finish their tea and sandwiches
then fold and unfold
their newspapers
When they return to work
the regular owl has ghosted in
to perch among the roof-struts
pebble-eyed and silent
The night-workers finish
between four and five
and leave separately
crossing the dark city
with the wet roads to themselves
Car radios are tuned to music
or a sports commentary
beamed from the antipodes
Someone on a bike
climbing a hill
snuggles into the wake
of the first milk-float

Full Circle

O
so I read
is the only letter
common to all sixty-six
alphabets of the world
Think of it
a baby cries
unswaddled
by circumflex or umlaut
lariats of smoke
from a last cigarette
loop the stop-go talk
of men settling to sleep
on the mattress of the pampas
Oedipus stumbles on
with owl eyes
apostrophizing
Bulgarian onomatopoeia
shares common ground
with Hebraic sweet nothings
and who knows
a nurse might fill in
a toe tag
surname first
and then my initial
without wondering
what it stood for

In the small town of Småpakke
not far from the border
in the early years of the century
the writer O
was being interviewed
The room had a view of the river
and as he spoke
the ferry could be seen
snouting its way across
to the Old Town
with a girl and a pram
and two tourists laughing
at the cheapness of the fare
and the handsbreadth
stretch of dull water
It's mostly I suppose
a matter of style
the writer said
His mind was wandering
First the ferry
and then this young lady
with her pen and notebook
and her hair up
showing the whiteness
of her ears
He crossed his legs
and addressed the ceiling
In 1718 there was
a complete change of style
in Prussian army uniform
known as the Stilbruch
Plainness

replaced dressiness
A tendril of hair
broke free and brushed
the page as she wrote
He stood up and walked
past her chair
to the window
Or take the two sorts
of houses in this town
The stone Valhallas
you see over there
were built for the so-called
plank aristocracy
the owners of the wood-mill
The wooden ones are for the workers
plain and simple
Had his fingers
touched her shoulder
The ferry was on its way back

The ferry was on its way back
I thought there was dirt or blood
crossing the surface of my eye
and blinked and blinked and saw
it was birds high up
swimming dots
Someone was playing a fiddle
as the ferry nuzzled to the quay
see-saw variations
on the national anthem
The old tunes
persistent as genes
will outlive us all
There's the schoolteacher
the town's human clock
walking home for lunch
and then returning on the dot
to the school inside the fortress
The fortress that won this place
a whole line to itself in the anthem
by withstanding siege
and sending the enemy
back across the border
Now it's us who slip over
for the summer sales or for a change
from a town that's had the luck
not to grow
You can tell the cars just returned
by the daytime blaze of headlights
stipulated by their law

Stipulated By Their Law
she would write
is a book of twists and turns
written in a denuded style
No
She should begin with him
Denuded
The horse had stopped
She was home
The driver asked for a fare
that seemed risibly cheap
and wouldn't be tipped
Father was outside
painting the flagpole
laid flat from a pivot in its base
She followed the fresh white paint
to the tapering end
knots and grain still showing
this had once been a tree
Mother has the kettle on
he said then resumed
his tongue-tip peeping out
Scratched music filled the hall
Her mother smiled at her and went on
waving her arms from the chair
half-conductor half-dancer
The kettle was nearly boiling
She lifted it off
Five minutes to cool
She stood there the whole time
quite still
music all round her like soft rain
still feeling inside her
a dipping and swaying
like someone newly arrived on land

Like someone newly arrived on land
the glassblower swung from side to side
clamping the tube to his mouth
and puffing from it a red bubble
molten with anger
and lengthening like slow elastic
The writer was often found
here in the Old Town
after one of his parties had ended
with the floor strewn with glass
Today though he wanted a present
Perhaps this bowl
which he could see
brimming with paper
quickly written envelopes and letters
He had it wrapped and hurried out
There was a live concert at four
to mark National Day
As usual there'd been flags everywhere
even on his taxi
He carefully put down the package
he'd send it tonight with a note
and then tuned in
He was soon away
jerking in his chair
he thought oddly
like a galvanist
What would a galvanist be doing
in the small town of Småpakke

The Phrenologist's Head

Is this how I'll end
a bald skull
on an attic shelf
porcelain skin
divided up
and labelled with attributes
Memory
the Moral and Ethical Region
Acumen
and Eventuality
Why should the centre of my head
be labelled Eventuality
If I cared to look
through the skylight
I'd see chimney-cowls
idling in the wind
turning this way and that
like the generals at Waterloo
but my eyes are blandly unseeing
as smooth and calm as grapes
and under the left one
stuck there on its own
like a name on a boat
is Language

Synopticon

for my father

The smell of ink
and fresh papyrus
He has finished
He unrolls the scroll
the length of his room
then walks alongside it
Seven paces
A life
lives
life and death
in seven sandalled paces
He has been writing for a week
and he has finished
He rubs his eyes
with small crushed hands
then sits under the window
looking at the scroll
a river of white
in the sunshine flooding
Alexandria
Antioch
or Rome

If Mark
was used by Matthew and Luke
for the events of Jesus' life
the source of the teachings
may have been a lost handbook
known by the symbol
Q
The German for source
is *Quelle*
and this symbol
is usually attributed
to Wellhausen
Lightfoot however
traces it back to Robinson
who said the first source
Mark
merely wrote down the words
of Peter
Thus the first source became
P
and the second or handbook
Q

Was he martyred
in Alexandria
only in legend
or was he martyred
for real
bound
dragged through the streets
to the precipice
known as Bucellus
Did they mock
his small clumsy hands
They mocked the broken hands
of Victor Jara
poet guitarist and singer
The tongue of fire
is torn out
No songs of Zion
And having broken his hands
they killed him

Q contains
wheat lilies grass trees
foxes lambs vipers chickens
Q contains
weddings loaves fishes
threshing lamps millstones
Q contains
ovens money sandals
music gifts children
Q contains

Colobodactylus
This Latin adjective
meaning stumpy-fingered
and applied to Mark
in an early text
has a number of glosses
His small hands
were congenital
He was a Levite
and had disfigured himself
to avoid being made a priest
The word applied not to him
but to his gospel
either because of the loss
of its ending
or because of the style
which purists find
blunt and awkward
Colobodactylus

Peter's interpreter
his hermeneut
Mark
now has more than one
hermeneut of his own
from the Germans
Bleek and Weiss
to the English
Abbot with his argument
unfairly apocopated
and the Oxford canon
whose overlooking
Ur-Marcus
was dubbed
Streeter's Fatal Omission

Come to bed
No
Come to bed
No
Her hand is tight
on his robe
He slips out of it
and flees
His original coat
of many colours
is now a bare few
red face
black hair
and the tan bobbing
of buttocks
Holding his robe
she falls back
Ah she sighs
Ah

Is that man with a cello
Hitchcock
Only a glimpse
and already the plot's
hurried on
The man met by the disciples
bearing a pitcher of water
is it Mark
When Jesus is arrested
he's followed by a yonge man
in Tyndale's version
cloothed in lynnen
apon the bare
Is it Mark
or as he's grabbed
and flees naked
is it just an echo
from Genesis
Torches and shouts fade
Slow dawn
That large petal
on the ground
turns out to be an ear

The Censor Dreams

On the window-sill
of the censor's house
was a chimney-cowl
an ornament
with the cachet
of past use
All around the house
the land lay silent
under the democracy
of snow
Persistent journeys
filled the fields
silently cluttering paths
till snow fell again
and smoothed out
the rustic tramlines
left by skis
The censor dreamt
of sperm
beading a face
On the morning tram
a young woman
wiped away tears
as she read of the rites
for Gerhardsen
thousands queueing
to pay their respects
and the King bowing
to the coffin
of the socialist
The younger a country is

thought the censor
the less it has
to be ashamed of
At his stop he stepped off
into a splash
dun snow
outstaying its welcome
Unlacing his boots at work
he thought of corsets
Today's offering
included a tram
in flames
He remembered the war
Standing Is Forbidden
When Seats Are Vacant
You could hate the enemy
but not snub him
Yet what's the worth
of enforced respect
He stared blind at the screen
the atonements of smoke
reeling skyward

Necropolis

Abraded and blinded
by a poisoned rain
the head of Minerva
on the library roof
has a consort of pigeons
Shit cakes the skylights
The single librarian
sleepwalking
shelves and shelves
of dust
picks at the scabs
of her nipples
The single reader
laughs noiselessly
blind head
thrown back
fingers flowing on
down the page

Listen to me
Listen to me
A sucker-mouth
breathing words
Listen
In out in out
a quick chain
of bubbles
only breaking
on the surface
only breaking
on your ears
Listen to me
Listen

The mirror factory's
brass band
is in full swing
in a room
lined with mirrors
The conductor's smile
tarnishes
as a saw
whines outside
Lopped cypresses crack
Trumpets quicken
Mirrors shimmer
The two bands race
first one ahead
then the other

The metal boy
thrusts
rigid arms
at the night sky
Is he tired and stretching
Is he wounded
At his feet
a duck potters blindly
in shallow water
Trees confer
Wind brushes
grass uphill
At the top
floodlights can be seen
across the city
Stars are lost
in the domed glare
and the moon fades
The wind sickens
with shouts

Because of the cuts
the school
hires out its fields
to a local stable
A boy watches
four whipped horses
gallop by
Torn grass and clods
arc up
and patter down
A handbell rings
in the playground
thinly
above drumming
hooves

Waves dun
at the sea-wall's base
Great heads of foam rear
dull white in the dark
Choose two pebbles
small and flat
Walk past the angler
with a storm-lamp
inside the calyx
of his umbrella
Slide through shingle
to the dark beyond
Lie down
Put the pebbles
on your eyes
Wait for the sea
to wash them off

DTs on Oliver's Island

Islands. Islands. Levels of sky-spilt light
on the flat wet sand at Pendine.
The Hayes Island snack-bar where you're trying
to outstare the Friend of Freedom's bronze arse,
your blown-rose mouth hugger-mugger with a teacup
and your chin smeared with mustard. The wind shifts
and you sit four-square in the public smell
of hops, the half-tang half-pall hung over Cardiff.
Here's to Skull Attack, its bouncy barrels
and whiffs of metal in the punters' brains,
and here's to the putto who pissed his pants,
the fat fly blundering in honey.

And here. The bridge booming with commuters as you row
    out
a boat loaded with booze lifted from London nobs
to a squat and shaggy island named, who knows,
for some Cromwellian rout, shouts over water,
water as black as knicker-elastic, peered into
as you drift, your face trembling, wavy: Narcissus
pouting round a fag-end.

Page Turner

Amongst all this passion
and precision, order
and fury, he retains
the tight-lipped plaster calm
of a venerable bust –
genius furrowing
its white brows at the name
embossed on its base – then
a casual guillotine
of cuff lifts into air,
the pianist submits
and the page sighs over,
a handkerchief waved once
before utter rapids
tumble about our ears
with him sitting unmoved,
the music embodied
and looking out at us.

The Composer's Ear-Trumpet

Pick me up. Put me to your ear.
No. The other way. Are you deaf?
Now, you should be able to hear
baton-taps and then the uncoiling clef

of the old tunes,
fury, fugue, double-basses like sea-swell,
molten brass, staid bassoons,
the old music caught in a shell.

A voice cries from a dead planet.
Shouting through clouds of hair-powder,
it's obdurate, deaf as granite:
'Louder. Louder. Louder.'

Chorus

for Tomas Lieske

Power wavers on its imperial plinth,
the rocket fizzles out to a burnt stick.
I'm happy with my lot: obscurity,
bland sunlight dawdling along empty streets,
a front door untroubled by the postman
and a life like water in a rain-butt.
And once the easy years have seeped away,
I'll enjoy the calm, anonymous death
denied to the powerful and famous,
the men who die known to all but themselves.

The Procurator's Last Posting

Voices at daybreak: the spurned
rise from earth in the new clothes
gifted them by rime as they slept.
The breath of words joins the hiss and steam
of pissers against trees, the levelling
of liquid over hard ground.
A red-tiled empire slowly breaks
from the rind of night and extras
throng the vomitories of day,
crossing the fields in ones and twos
and muttering on the outskirts.

★

Autumn. Solemnities for dead August
haunt the woods with plumb September rain.
Squall-stunned earth, naked and sad,
subsides like a beast
under the slaughterer's hammer.
Day trails back to its byre,
a lone bell coming home
with infuriating slowness.
The best time of your life
is this stretch of hoof-socketed mud.

★

Fissured air swishes
with the studious sweep
of a god's wings,
the moon-on-water face
and blanched smile
seen and gone
into a gap in the air
like a daytime light
lit and then doused.

★

What's that thudding from the wharf?
Barrels.
So they work at night?
Tonight and every night.
Under guard?
Not your usual guard,
your boiled briskets in dull armour –
this one's the business.
One man?
One.
Is he empowered?
Imperially, absolutely and imperially empowered.
Is that allowed?
Why ask me? Why not him?

Professor

She has a sixth finger
she fills from a bottle.
It can pause and then dive
like the stoop of a hawk.
Her mind hovers, then dives.
Palisaded by files,
reviewing the endless
cannon-fodder of books,
her voice surprises you –
generous ricochets
instead of bombardment.
Home time. The door opens
and her cat skips downstairs
to the Staff Club. Four gins,
the last sloshing her dress.
Behind thick spectacles,
book-dimmed eyes flit at you
like fish butting their tanks.

Washing the Corpse

They had grown familiar with him. Yet
as the draughty kitchen narrowed and leapt
in nervy lamplight, he still kept
his anonymity, aloof and wet.

Knowing nothing of his past, they threw one off
as they worked, their fictions as deft
as the way they washed him. One had to cough
and the vinegar-soaked sponge was left

on his face. The other woman stopped too.
Water gathered on a scrubbing brush, then dispersed
drop by drop while his hand, clenching and blue,
clenched tighter as if he knew,
but had to prove, he was beyond thirst.

And he proved it. Embarrassed,
they cleared their throats and worked.
On the wall behind them, harassed
and harassing shadows grappled and jerked

like a ship swarming with boarders
till the women had done what they'd aimed
to do. Stark night was framed
by uncurtained windows. And lying there unnamed,
clean and naked, he gave orders.

Exempla

The two women strutting into the Chanel shop
had the equine hauteur and carriage
you find in Gainsborough and Reynolds,
that high-protein centuries-old certainty,

just as back home on the Byres Road
you'd meet a soft high-coloured face
straight out of Raeburn, Lady This or That
long dead and now working in the baker's.

Miss McCullen always sat up on top,
a nondescript spy taking comfort
from the conductor's uncomplicated code –
one ring for stop, two for go – and eavesdropping.

'Topped herself. Jumped from the Whispering Gallery.
A hundred and five feet. She lived on her own.
When the coppers broke in, it smelled so bad
they thought she'd done someone in. She died on the
    chairs.'

Waiting at her place in the Reading Room,
her gaze flitted upwards to the book-stacks.
Thirty feet . . . Sixty . . . Costive light struggled
over the sills . . . Eighty . . . Something thumped on her
    desk.

'Beg pardon, Love. It's the books you wanted.'
Head down, she drew them to her, nodded her thanks.
'Don't worry, Love, it might never happen.'
He left as she spread her pencils, a fan of points.

How broad the eye of a needle is, how capacious!
Miss McCullen looked through sampler
after sampler: a whole, known world
where Adam and Eve are always allotted

the left and right of a tree always wound
with a snake's anti-clockwise coils,
where crucifixion's formal agony is semaphored
by the ends of a loincloth pointing up and down,

where Ellen Parker, jailed for drunkenness,
shares a cell with a mother and baby
and makes them a sampler from her headscarf,
using her own hair for thread

and where this seventeenth-century figure
is yet to be explained – a naked boxer
with a crazed face collapsed into a grin
who offers a bouquet like a right hook.

Five o'clock and Miss McCullen
has taken the point off all her pencils,
writing and sketching with the bent head
of any seamstress, visionary or submissive.

With the light outside grown surly,
she sits in the circus-ring cast by her lamp,
deaf at last to the buses' bells
and to the traffic's whispering, whispering.

Old Country Radical

Quavered promulgation
of ideas regardless
of their reception. Talk.
Talk. Talk. An Oxfam suit.
A hunched nose repeating
the seventy-year stoop.
The loud nailed stride crossing
lanes, roads, fences, counties —
a pair of compasses
swallowing the atlas.
The half-life of clippings
and notebooks, news and plots
from other people's lives.
Somewhere a wife, deadened
by TV's narcotic,
waits to be remembered
like that old article
he really must finish.

Oliver and Tone Have Moved to Chelsea

A man sits in a blossom-flecked Daimler
and reads the *FT*, stroking his wattles.
All the pinks! It's spring in car-phone country
and every bird's buttonholing the sky
with the latest prices. Worms are up, up!
A key turns, setting pistons whispering
on a sheen of irreproachable oil.
High above the city, a plane draws out
a slow burr of sound like a glass-cutter
scoring a window. One tap and you're through.

★

Assayed a pint of Old Rebarbative
down at the Arts with young What's-his-face.
Said he was stuck with his novel. *Pig's Ear*.
Stuck. Need a JCB to get unstuck.
Rappaport fining down the beer too much.
Leaves a taste of Brasso the day after
on the higher reaches of the palate.
Remember it from a boy when I sucked
one of Uncle's buttons all afternoon.
Suck, suck, suck. Him droning on about Haig.

★

Phylacteries guarding what's most precious,
burglar alarms line the mews. His home's wheeled,
his life portable. What's the going rate
for this des. res. in SW10:
a shopping-trolley crammed with all mod cons
(newspapers, blankets, carpet remnants, rope,
sticks, old shoes, a Japanese umbrella . . .)?
Parked by a new flat's security gates,
eyes veering and orbiting, he mutters
to no one in a stricken falsetto.

                    ★

Elsewhere is the huge impress of action —
windows glaring under a frown of smoke,
panic, the sudden clotting of traffic,
the struggle with leggings in the cramped cab
as the fire engine, cornering at speed,
slews out its tremendous spoor of water —
while here, the automatic doors rattling
placidly into place, is empty calm:
a concrete hall bare but for the paired shoes,
the black slip-ons left behind on the floor.

                    ★

A table upended on the river's
mud-slabbed margin or a power station,
its four cream chimneys Doric and defunct?
Under the bridge. Then the hospital, right,
aligns clocktower, flag and gold-topped pillar;
left, the park's incongruous pagoda.
Two more bridges. Low tide's all roofs and spires;
high tide sees the city walled and peopled.
And here's the harbour where Money lives.
Money and his mistress, Ease. Ahoy there!

★

From the top of our street, the goat in boots
raises his glass to the man in the moon's
bulging cheeks and tankard at the bottom.
All day long, the torpid planes flaunt themselves
from roof to roof, sliding down to Heathrow.
Our bell-push marked 'Top Flat', our mail 'care of . . .',
we're subtenants on the sly, hesitant
sippers at this new wine we've just opened,
eyes ritually fixed as we make the toast
in silence: care of luck, and each other.

Spanish Dancer

Like one of those old sulphur matches,
a lucifer, self-haloed in your hand
and spurting white before it catches,
she starts and the circled crowd watches
the dance feed on itself till it's fanned

into flame, sudden and bright.

The eyes set the hair alight.
The dress burns higher and higher,
red-hot, committed to the fire
from which, rearing like startled rattlesnakes,
each naked arm clicks and shakes.

Then, as if the fire were too tight a fit,
she rolls it up and, like a skin, casts it:
contemptuous, a Grand Signior
whose slave grovelling on the floor
is the fire, still burning, not yet dead –
till she, triumph almost complete,
a smiling mask on a lifted head,
stamps it out with tiny, tidying feet.

Temples

Sucked down the narrow streets off the canal
by the capillary action of lust,
men veer from pavement to pavement, nervy,
tense, eyes harassed and jumpy as pinballs;
or, the younger ones, too loud, too certain.

A corner tout offers hard-core action,
the same scraps of language juggled from Dutch
to English and back, finding no takers
among men sick of being spectators,
one hand pocketed on a bulge of notes.

A woman walks to work, led by her dog –
a canine Cupid, glossy and ribboned,
its lead the same shade as her bikini –
her thigh-flesh a flurry of opposites
kept going by the hard strut of high heels.

And the lights come on in the small windows,
revealing the bold and the dejected
and the two sitting out on their doorsteps,
the Dayglo stretch of swimwear showing up
brown-black skins, long wrists idling as they chat.

This packed insouciance of head and haunch
fills each small square of animated light –
calendar for a secular Advent
where each saint, blessed and all-too-human, knows
the only coming is that of money.

Education Debate at the Burrell

Two exhibits from Glasgow's Burrell Collection
(seen at a time when the principal of one of the city's
universities was advocating the replacement of student
grants by a loan scheme): a painting by Théodule Ribot
(1823–1891), an artist forced into the role of family
breadwinner at sixteen when his father died and
often able to paint only at night by lamplight; and
a *shawabti*, an Egyptian figurine buried with
the mummy to serve as a stand-in should the dead
person be called upon to work in the next world.

Blue. Bottle blue. Blowfly blue.
The bluebottle's thousand-coned eye
scanning the dead lustre
of its own gun-metal shanks;
eager buzzwords
and an egg-heavy flight
pregnant with fever.

Dead Nile blue. Death blue.

Blue air humming
from a clapped-out pylon
gorged with juice, gorged
and crackling with light.

The death-glaze blue
of a *shawabti*
stuck in a case,
the call to work
with sand and seed
going unheard –
or millennia
knocking on glass

and the required response
unheard:
'Here I am!'

★

Théodule Ribot
works by day
for a mirror maker,

goldfish eyes
gaping and pursing
as he gilds and gilds

scrolls and putti
framing the future
of the Paris rich.

The workshop suddenly
slid under sunlit water . . .
or just the shivering

commercial light
of pot after pot
of gold paint?

Back home, past midnight,
five smoky moons
circle his easel.

The still-life won't stay still,
black wavering into grey,
dreaming of daylight.

Can he believe his eyes?
Yes, if he had time
and one more lamp.

★

With her awkward nose and square, stubborn brow,
she stands – holding a book in front of her
and, forgotten under an arm,
the dead plumes of a duster –
like some workaday Justice
weighing Knowledge and Labour.
This is her learning: transgression,
something taken from the master's table
(its funereal green cloth
cluttered with bright new editions
dipped into, half-read, tossed aside
and waiting to be tidied)
when the front door has shut
and she's alone with the confederacy of clocks
and the starched crackle of pigeons
plumping down to crumbs on the lawn.
The awkwardness, the persistence
of the attempt to understand!

★

And the necessity of it.
In Ribot's *Domestique Studieuse*,
she emerges from the subterfuge of shadow
just as she emerged now for me
(reading of more education cuts)
from memory into meaning:
'Here I am!'

something given (or taken) – like knowledge –
not bought, something persistent,
a pattern of light, of words, of experience,
ready to stand forward and say:
'Here I am!'

'Here I am!'

Encore

'And then your sonnet, "Birds in Time of Drought",'
said the journalist, 'what's all that about?'
Fag-smoke blossomed on the old poet's breath.
'If I had to say . . . love and rain and death.'

What else beside these: death and rain and love?
Each word sent out in hope like Noah's dove
returning empty-beaked, flying in vain
above lost woods and hills levelled with rain . . .

'If I had to say . . . rain and love and doubt.'
The cigarette broke as he stubbed it out.
'You're undecided between doubt and death?'
The old man called, coughed, and called again: 'Beth!'

The wife came in. Her voice was low, devout.
'You'll have to go now. It's late. He's worn out.'
She smoothed the pillow. 'Everything's there, love,
pills in the bottom drawer, pencils above.'

The door closed. A last hoot from a far train
and the birdless air fell silent. Then rain.
Then the sounds of quick scribbling and slow breath.
He had the title . . . love and rain and death.

Home

Beyond the striving tump of the ant-hill
and across the meadow thinking
of becoming marsh, you return at last

to this slew of timbers,
roof-beams grounded in grass
and, in the one wall still standing,

the door and its rusted padlock
that stood the test,
whatever test it was.

The Lost Bracelet

the sky's breathing snow
and here we are in your bed
by the wide white windows
in the quiet mouth of the world

dreaming together
words diffused into music
stations tuned too close
for the dial to distinguish

in your dream you're losing again
the gold bracelet I gave you
and returning again
to all the sad shops

did it slip unseen
with a glove from your wrist
where will it be
when you wake

whose body is this
you're so close to
crouched and smoothing
down and suddenly down

to the level of a lake
where the only noise
in a world dumb with white
is the quick shush of skis

and where fish dreaming
in their bed of ice
see sunlight circle
in water like gold

The Cultural Workers' First Week

for Irene and Thorbjørn

eagles turn above the dead headland
with its wrecked iodine factory
and water in a concrete tank deepened
across decades to the glossed black of marble

where once they hauled in seaweed
and sent out the sack-heavy boats
timbers reduced to charcoal now point
to what's left of a roof

rusted cogs engage on air
and coastal grasses win by attrition
sure of the logistics
of wind and salt

on the orange rectory's white-painted porch
facing the sea across a garden of nettles
and a flagless pole the new couple
takes coffee and strews the floor with fag-ends

that won't be swept till the brush is unearthed
from the boxes and cases the trumpet and six guitars
flown two hours from the capital to here
where civic shields boast puffins or stockfish

the future emerges piecemeal from newspapers
crockery pictures an angel whose wing they'll reglue
and claims the twenty rooms and two hollow staircases
echoing less and less of the past

they tack up maps their parish of performance
and discussion three hours drive from end to end
past graveyards where adults are buried closest
to the mountain children closest to the sea

on Saturday the fuses blow and in the evening
a candle makes its way downstairs window by window
to join the oil-lamp lent by the neighbour
and in the soft old light they eat and drink

Magnificat

Debts were incurred early, the body feeding first not on mother's milk, but her blood. After the colourful entry – the shocked head fisting at the world – transfusion had seemed the last thing this crimson screamer needed, but transfusion it was. Who would have thought the young man had so little blood in him?

You are what you see. Two rows of terraced houses like the teeth of a zip. A road-sweeper works his way to his cart in a brisk parley of bristles. A boy stumbles after with a mimic broom twice his size: first steps in the kindergarten of the gutter.

'Rosemary' and 'Dreadnought': tracing the leak in the roof, the twitchy torch finds the underside of each tile named. A recession of ranked names, the same couple doomed over and over in the register. Cramped air flutters, there's the scrape of claws on the tiles outside, then the considered cooing of pigeons. Do you, Dreadnought, take this woman, Rosemary . . .

Miles inland, following the river, gulls screech around the chimney-pots. Memory booms on the wind: the pier with its weed-slimed struts and the queasy sump of the sea; the old mine that's now a collection-box, danger-red and studded with defused nipples; the rub they're given for luck, or out of nostalgia, before the slot for charity is found and fed.

What's as empty as an empty bandstand? Crossing the park, the afternoon walk reaches its usual end. This is the orangery in winter, bare space keeping its counsel about the cupids crushed under empty urns. White silence. Echoes, like oranges, are only imaginary. The window returns a washed-out face. A kite dives earthward, failure corroborated (after the necessary interval) by a bump.

Christmas Eve at the Goat and the verger's saying little, head turned aside to funnel fag-smoke at the ceiling and to watch the women. Scalloped in a bodice of red velvet, breasts are served up like dollops of Botticelli. An hour after last orders the bell at St John's tolls insistently, the proven air found pure. Jerking the rope, the verger thinks of velvet.

The tide of what was love ebbs to duty or pity. That hat on that face seems not quite right, like Madagascar on the map, coincidental to Africa. Such a cold comparison. Are you what you see? A cold eye taking in these hands, their bluish tinge in winter as your blood grudgingly makes its rounds. Migration charges the square's municipal air with starlings, sudden soot swarming over civic porticoes. Twilight's jittery with static twitter. It could be distress or praise.